NATIONAL GEOGRAPHIC

School Publishing

Measurement

Tessa Patel

PICTURE CREDITS
Cover, 7, Myrleen Ferguson Cate/PhotoEdit, Inc.; 1, 9, Tony Freeman/PhotoEdit, Inc.;
2, 12, 13 (above), 15 (left), 16 (right), 18 (above right), David Young-Wolff/
PhotoEdit, Inc.; 4 (left), Felicia Martinez/PhotoEdit, Inc.; 4 (above right), 8, 10,
16 (left), 19 (above), Getty Images; 4 (below right), APL/Corbis; 5 (all), 15 (right),
18 (left and below right), Photolibrary.com; 6, Michael Newman/PhotoEdit, Inc.;
9, 11, 13, Gaston Vanzet; 11, Paul Bricknell/Dorling Kindersley; 13 (below), Ibis for
Kids Australia; 14, Richard Hutchings/PhotoEdit, Inc.; 17, Dennis MacDonald/age
fotostock; 19 (below), Peter Anderson/Dorling Kindersley.

Produced through the worldwide resources of the National Geographic Society, John
M. Fahey, Jr., President and Chief Executive Officer; Gilbert M. Grosvenor, Chairman
of the Board; Nina D. Hoffman, Executive Vice President and President, Books and
Education Publishing Group.

PREPARED BY NATIONAL GEOGRAPHIC SCHOOL PUBLISHING
Steve Mico, Executive Vice President and Publisher, Children's Books and Education
Publishing Group; Marianne Hiland, Editorial Director; Lynnette Brent, Executive
Editor; Michael Murphy and Barbara Wood, Senior Editors; Nicole Rouse, Editor;
Bea Jackson, Design Director; David Dumo, Art Director; Shanin Glenn, Designer;
Margaret Sidlosky, Illustrations Director; Matt Wascavage, Manager of Publishing
Services; Sean Philpotts, Production Manager.

MANUFACTURING AND QUALITY MANAGEMENT
Christopher A. Liedel, Chief Financial Officer; Phillip L. Schlosser, Vice President;
Clifton M. Brown III, Director.

BOOK DEVELOPMENT
Ibis for Kids Australia Pty Limited.

Published by the National Geographic Society
1145 17th Street, N.W.
Washington, D.C. 20036-4688

Product No. 4W1005055

ISBN-13: 978-1-4263-5051-1
ISBN-10: 1-4263-5051-1

2010 2009 2008
5 6 7 8 9 10 11 12 13 14 15

Printed in China

Contents

cup

stopwatch

ruler

4

What are these people measuring?
What measurement tools are they using?

tape measure

scale

Length, Width, and Height

Sometimes we want to find out how long something is. So we measure its length.

This boy is measuring the length of some yarn.

Sometimes we want to find out how wide something is. So we measure its width.

This girl is measuring the width of the door.

Sometimes we want to find out how high or tall something is. So we measure its height.

These students are using a measuring stick to measure height.

8

Units of Measurement

Length, width, and height can be measured in **inches** and **feet**.	Length, width, and height can be measured in **centimeters** and **meters**.

Estimating

We can estimate how long, wide, or tall something is.

I know I'm about 4 feet tall. So this door must be about 8 feet tall.

Weight

Sometimes we want to find out how heavy something is.
So we measure its weight.

Units of Measurement

Weight can be measured in **ounces** and **pounds**.	Weight can be measured in **grams** and **kilograms**.

bathroom scale

kitchen scale

Estimating Weight

We can estimate how heavy something is.

This bag of apples weighs about 2 pounds.

This bag of apples weighs about 1 pound.

Volume

Sometimes we want to measure the volume of something. Volume is the amount of space something takes up.

We use **teaspoons**, **tablespoons**, and **cups** to measure volume.

We use **pints**, **quarts**, and **gallons** to measure volume.

Sometimes we measure volume in **liters**.

We can estimate the volume of something.

I think it will take about 2 cups of water to fill this jar.

Temperature

Sometimes we want to find out
how hot or cold something is.
So we measure its temperature.

We measure temperature by using a thermometer. It tells the temperature in degrees.

degrees Celsius (°C)

degrees
Fahrenheit (ºF)

Sometimes a doctor measures
your temperature.

Temperature can be measured in
degrees Celsius and degrees Fahrenheit.

Time

We measure time by using clocks and calendars.
Time can be measured in seconds, minutes, and hours.
Time can be measured in days, weeks, months, and years.

minute hand

second hand

hour hand

month

day

date

There are 60 seconds in a minute.
There are 60 minutes in an hour.
There are 24 hours in a day.

We can measure how much time something takes. This timer shows how long it took the rider to finish the race.

hours

minutes

seconds

A calendar shows the month, the day, and the date.

17

market scale

measuring cup

doctor

18

There are many ways to measure things. Tell what is happening in these pictures.

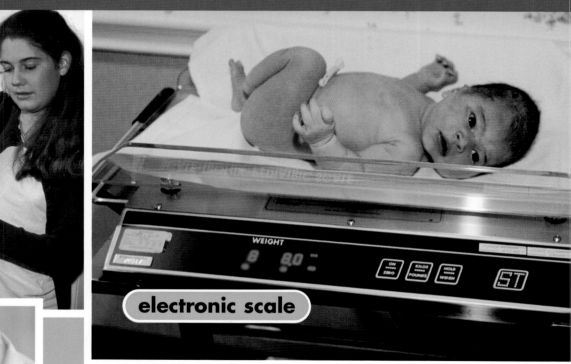

electronic scale

tape measure

inch
foot (feet)
centimeter
meter

ounce
pound
gram
kilogram

teaspoon
tablespoon
cup
pint
quart
gallon
liter

19

Picture Glossary

calendar

clock

measuring cup

ruler

scale

tape measure

thermometer